MOMENTS BEFORE MIDNIGHT

MOMENTS BEFORE MIDNIGHT

OREGON POETS WRITE FOR

ECOLOGICAL, SOCIAL, POLITICAL,

AND ECONOMIC JUSTICE

Bob Hill Publishing, LLC
JEFFERSON, ORE

Printed in the United States of America

Published by Bob Hill Publishing, LLC
Jefferson, Ore

ISBN 978-1-943780-20-4

February, 2018

First Printing

CONTENTS

FORWARD

This book was written by Oregon poets as a response to the unsettling political climate in this country and elsewhere. The authors of these works come from a diverse group in age and experience. Most are native-born Americans citizens who didn't choose which land to live in, while others did. In the end, all want to protect our country from the distressing changes that are taking place. And so, to put our money where our mouths are, all proceeds from the sale of this book will be donated to the ACLU to help that organization's continuing work of protecting our freedoms.

The title refers to the Doomsday Clock that ticks ever closer to the symbolic midnight that will bring about the Sixth Extinction by means of a manmade cataclysm, wherein many species of life will be forever lost. Scientists conceived of this as a way to graphically show how we are affecting our little planet, the only home we have in the immensity of the cosmos.

However, the clock is not a final determination because over the years the minute hand has moved close and then receded from the all-important tipping point at midnight.

The poets in this collection share the common attribute of living in Oregon, but their lives have taken unique paths. Represented in this book you will find many educators, artists, a chiropractor, an actor, novelists and more; people with an amazing array of view points and a substantial depth of talent. The poems have been influenced by background, gender, education, religion, and, of course, personal experience. In these pages you will find poems that speak of sadness, anger, outrage, disbelief and hope.

When the lives of millions of good people are impacted by the actions of a few who seem determined to take all they can without thought of giving back, who hoard wealth while grabbing still more, and are supporters of hate and seem to sell fear like a commodity, then we can't be quiet. Our words tell of sorrow and pain, and yet, as in any work of art, there are always visions of a better tomorrow.

It has been my privilege to edit this collection, as well as participate as a contributing poet. I want to thank everyone who sent in their poems and trusted Bob Hill Publishing, LLC, to represent them as they poured forth their outrage and courage.

Amalie Rush Hill

JENNIFER ROOD

Jennifer Rood teaches English in Southern Oregon. She is active in her union and supportive and proud of her husband and three children, all of whom volunteer in some way to make the community better. She has great friends, an awesome fig jam recipe, and a lot more life to live well.

About the poem: "Hope"

Musing one day about superheroes that we don't have but need, I wondered what a pragmatic optimist might carry in her utility belt that would always be the right tool to help her fight for justice. It made sense that she would always carry hope, and hope soon took the form of a knife, which has the power to carve out a new and better future for us all. When wielded well, hope is not just thought, but action. This poem was the result of those thoughts about what can result from active hope.

Hope

Keep it at your hip like a knife.
It is your best tool.
Do not forget that you carry it with you.
You have sheathed it in doubt,
which conceals its power. But do not forget.
Do not forget to take it out
and admire how it gleams.
It is yours.
Know it is yours to use.Use it.
Use it to pry open closed doors.
Use it to slice through old paradigms.
Use it to sever the pervasive patterns
of what has been
from the possibilities of what can be.
Use it to cleave injustice
from the body of the land and
from the experience of its people.
Use it to carve new monuments.
Use it to cut through the bone cage of fear
that surrounds your own heart
so you can free the doves that flutter there,
already beating their wings.
Take it with you into your future,
and into your children's future,
where you will build your best life,
with this, your best tool.

HOWARD W. ROBERTSON

Howard W. Robertson is a poet and fiction writer who lives in Eugene, Oregon. He has published ten books of poems, including *Hope Speaks* in 2016, and three books of fiction, including *Love in the Cretaceous* in 2017. He has won numerous literary awards, has been published in many literary journals, and has been anthologized often. Sustainability and ecology are major themes in both his poetry and his fiction.

For more about Howard, go to http://www.howardwrobertson.com/.

The Sixth Extinction

I'm a moray eel, I'm peering from
my hole / O, I'm a big red rooster,
 and I'm on the prowl / insomnia and
billowed sails, my love now plows
the moonless sea / the poet sings
with utmost candor, on the table
burns a candle / ice will bend you
like a branch, the night will toss you
on the roof / bacteria snatch genes,
promiscuously thrive / Anthropocene
despair finds one-point, breathes.

Ice—storm

I wear a tie-die of a scarlet dragonfly
/ the alder branches fall upon the
helpless house / the ice has gravitas,
the snow knows no restraint / except
for trouble and bad luck, we'd have
no luck tonight / so this is what it
sounds like, global warming, the big
branches breaking off the tallest trees
like cannons going off / my heart
already flits through a riparian forest
like a hundred-million years ago.

Cosmic drink

Alcohol is termed a toxin, literally
poison / drunk is termed intoxicated,
literally poisoned / sober is a song of
love divine, a spirit that forever
nurtures and embraces all things big
and small / the one vast vertebrate
idea develops through the many
hundred million years, the one great
sober thought of blue whales,
elephants, tyrannosaurs, apatosaurs,
iguanodons, giraffes, the unifying
concept that includes the geckos,
field mice, shrews, chameleons, pine
siskins, rainbow trout, the myriad
embodied variations huge or little on
the one same theme / the human
animal remains indifferent, becomes
enthralled, okay, perhaps inspired,
whatever, sees that we too are the
Universe / water, straight, no chaser.

PAUL SUTER

After college and university studies that began in 1963 (highlights – M.A. English, University of California, Berkeley; program preparing community college teachers of English, University of Nebraska), I taught composition and literature courses in the Denver Community College system from 1971 until 1973. In 1973, I was hired by the English department at Chemeketa Community College. There I taught basic writing to advanced composition; introductory fiction, drama and poetry; world literature; Shakespeare's plays; American literature. In the 1990's, I developed Chemeketa's first environmental literature course.

I retired from my teaching career at Chemeketa in 2010. Today my interests include much of what had been my life prior: family (three grandchildren now, whom my wife and I thoroughly enjoy); gatherings and events with friends and acquaintances, especially music, art and poetry; reading (nature and environmental selections, memoir, fiction, and poetry). I've covered much of Oregon, Washington and parts of Idaho and Montana by bicycle. I have written poems for years, but now I am doing so with much more focus and attention to the craft. I have read some of my poems locally and in Ashland—and I am revising and writing poems for consideration of publication.

"Cathedral" got its start in an "open writing time" hosted by Stephanie Lenox during her writer's residency (8/17) in the Annex Studio of the Bush Barn Art Center in Salem, Oregon.

I want to thank Stephanie, two Willamette University students and a fellow member of the Trillium Writers Group, who listened to me read revisions. Their feedback kept me alert to possibilities in the drafts.

Stephanie's prompt consisted of a triangulation of a Jim Harrison poem, "Sunlight," a 1300-word sentence by Joanne Avallon, and a specific prompt to "write a poem...(in which you) describe an image that allows you to make grand statements about time, mortality, the cosmos, etc." "Cathedral" is the result.

All elements of Stephanie's prompt played a part in my composing process. This result fulfilled a goal of Stephanie's residency —"to dispel the myth of the inspired writer composing in isolation." Further, during her residency, Stephanie questioned "the boundary between reality and the world we invent for ourselves. How are we changed by what we believe? Where is the line between invention and truth?"

Cathedral

> *after Jim Harrison's "Sunlight," which is set*
> *in the Salt Lake City airport and begins:*
> *"After days of darkness I didn't understand*
> *a second of yellow sunlight"*

I remember...O'Hare Airport in Chicago boasts
white, crystalline arches, glass walls,
sound quieted by these pliant constraints,
with travelers hushed into thoughtful corners
of their mind, slower rhythms,
even the late arriving ones,
the passage from one end of the terminal
to the other a time for reflection on childhood,
youth, making friends, maybe marriage,
perhaps children back home,
a neighborhood, the family dog, familiar parks,
their walkways, trees and summer flowers,
their winter skate rinks,
places where friends and family gathered
to remember a companion or uncle who has passed.
Then a moment to read the latest news
of hurricanes in Texas and Florida
or clashes in the streets of Charlottesville,
or suicide killings with truck or car in Paris,
time stopped for victims,
people who gave their lives
to family and friends, rich lives
rooted in places
that reach back thousands of years,

and briefly the O'Hare travelers stop,
look out through the crystal glass
to the immense blue of a cloudless day
and imagine unknown destinations—
among nebulae, stars, galaxies, planets—
and re-invented stories told by fellow passengers
on the endless flights that will be theirs.

JENNIFER ROLLINGS

Jennifer Rollings is a proud Oregon writer living in the Willamette Valley. Her poetry has been featured by Clementine Unbound, UnLost Journal, Every Writer, and WordWrights! magazine.

"The Lion's Walk" was written in the run-up to the 2016 US elections, and is meant to embody the complex quality of feminine leadership capability.

"Blackberrying" addresses the many conflicting emotions I feel about the natural world these days, especially while doing any form of gardening.

The Lion's Walk: A Pantoum for Progress

The lion's doomed to failure in a cage.
But you tell me most will terrify before one,
and there's seldom more than one given the stage,
no lion really wants to share the sun.
But you tell me most will terrify before one,
so I tell the lion frank her odds, her chance,
no lion really wants to share the sun
she can read the signs herself and at a glance.
So I tell the lion frank her odds, her chance.
She returns my frankness, bright with glaring eyes.
She can read the signs herself, and at a glance,
Those who back down are those whom I despise.
She returns my frankness. Bright, with glaring eyes.
Who cares for lollygaging anyway?
Those who back down are those whom I despise.
Like it or not, the Lion has her say.
Who cares for lollygagging anyway,
They cannot stop a draft, or raise a wage.
Like it. Or not. The Lion has her say.
The Lion's doomed to failure in a cage.

Blackberrying

Beginning my annual battle against their spiraling vines,
wearing the heavy gloves, swinging the shears,
I have my usual twinge of guilt.
Yes, they've overgrown the driveway,
sharp teeth swiping the paint from cars.
Their fruit has withered and fallen,
usefulness gone another year.
Yet it seems dangerous,
cutting down living things for our convenience.
True, I get annoyed.
Is this not our land to steward as we need?
But sometimes I think this is how a curse unfurls,
sinks its claws into a family's future.
When they are all excised, next comes the bundling.
Then the bundles into burn pile,
while I dwell on the Inquisition.
Across my cheek, a branch rebels,
extracts a scarlet reciprocity.
I look up at clouds,
as if to apologize.
I wonder, will there be a way
to balance these scales again?

AMALIE RUSH HILL

Born to artist parents, I drew on every piece of paper I laid hands on, made up stories to illustrate and was always reading books. I have written four science fiction novels in the *The Ambolaja Series*, numerous short stories, essays, and much poetry. I intend to continue writing and learning as long as I am able.

I live with my multi-generational family in the country. Rural living was a new experience for me when we moved out of Salem in 1995, but I love being surrounded by nature. My recent poetry and short stories reflect the influence of the abundant life around me and the gifts of inspiration it gives me.

Is it Too late?

This poem is a reminder that the world, after WWII, began to slowly morph into the corporatocracy we have now. Life was never "Ozzie and Harriet" or "Father Knows Best"—those were manufactured myths still believed by many people, cultural leftovers along with the myths of the glorified Old South and the Wild West. But the future has yet to be written...

Inauguration Day 2016

The inspiration for this poem came to me as I was walking down our dead end road on January 21, 2017. I walked nearly everyday and the road spoke to me many times. On the day of the poem, it revealed that what may look glittery is most times merely a coverup of something unremarkable.

A Choice of Endings in Three Acts

This poem is about hope, despite the title. There is so much we have to be thankful for and we often forget acknowledge it.

Is It Too Late?

Having grown up during the
Atomic cold war years
I had grown used to the idea of
Annihilation
A nuclear war would most assuredly
Have destroyed life, but not all of it
And what was left might have
Closely resembled the monsters
Depicted in 1950-era movies
The giant ants, Godzilla and other
Mutated lifeforms
But the Cold War eventually thawed
And we learned
That even ideological differences
Need not be the end of the world
We grew up believing there had to
Be a better way
But instead we got
"Better Living Through Chemistry"
And other corporate slogans
To brainwash the public into
Submission in a far more
Insidious process than Communism
Had ever done
And now we face another kind of
Annihilation
Except this one, fueled by
Disinformation, ignorance and
Long ago planted mind-bombs

Has taken on a life of its own
Is it too late to stop this headlong
Race to the finish line?
What was set into motion centuries ago
By curious and inventive humans
Has grown into a kind of monster
The very epitome of Godzilla
Rising from the depths of the sea
To wreak havoc on the world

Of men and his technology
This time there are no enemies
To negotiate with
Or with whom to roll back hostilities
To reach detente
This time it is our own hubris
Rapacity and denial of the effects
Of our actions
That accelerate the early demise of
The planet's biosphere
The submersion of continents
And most importantly,
The loss of polar Ice Caps
And thawing permafrost
That releases ever more carbon dioxide
And methane
This changes everything
And will eventually kill almost all life
Except for maybe cockroaches
But certainly the tiny tardigrade
Will live on

A most alien-looking little thing
Able to withstand cosmic radiation
And extreme temperatures from
Sunlike to nearly absolute zero
For short periods of time
And they can survive for thirty years
Without food or water
Is this what we have chosen,
This microscopic animal
Much like those monsters
Conceived by film makers
To leave behind on a world
Once teeming with
Diverse and beautiful life?
Is this what we truly want
To be our legacy, our progeny?
Is it too late to change course?

A Choice of Endings in Three Acts

Act One:
In the end,
it all comes down to a sincere
desire that no one is allowed
to destroy life on our planet.
The politics are important, too
I suppose
but there are so many things to be done
Now
After climate change approaches
critical mass
that all important tipping point
after the temperature and the seas
rise too high
when disease becomes pandemic
and plants and animals die off,
then,
politics will no longer
be of much importance
If the soil, sterilized by herbicides,
can no longer nurture seeds,
if the water is tainted,
if the oceans and tundra belch methane
making the air unbreathable,
then
whichever political side you are on,
it will seem as though
a debate would only be
a futile and reckless

waste of oxygen.

Act Two:
I ask of you,
and I hope you will
ponder this in your heart
This plot that I have written,
this woeful tale of a dying Earth,
this imminent future
with a tragic last act
has been based on your
disbelief in science and facts,
your unwillingness to accept change
and if you help elect
Politicians
who won't respond to the basic needs
of people
who won't wean themselves
away from petroleum and dark money
who pander to billionaires and polluters,
who slaver over unspoiled land
to exploit,
if this is the beginning of the end,
who will you appeal to for help then?
Who will come to pull you
out of the toxic sea,
out of the rivers of burning chemicals?
There will be no FEMA response
for this disaster,
no last-minute heroic rescue,
no music playing as the credits roll.

This will be an end to which
you will say,
Wow, I never saw that coming!
And what an ending it will be
smelling of death and rot,
turning the planet
into an unending charnel house
while empty dry winds howl like banshees
across scorched and barren landscapes

Act Three:
When the last images fade
and the movie screen goes blank
in the darkened theatre,
but the house lights don't come
Up
That means
it really is the end.
But should I be proven wrong
and this dire vision of a lost future
turns out to be unfounded
then I shall sing joyfully
with thanks
as the blackbird of song
With praise for the morning
and the dawn of a New Day

Inauguration Day 2016

While walking down the lane
After a morning rain
The sun peeked out from behind
The clouds
Setting the flat grey
Road a-glitter
As though paved
With diamonds
And when the sun was
Once again obscured behind
Clouds
The road more closely
Resembled
Empty words
And broken promises
Exposing it to be
What it truly is,
Asphalt
Ordinary gravel and tar

CHARLES R CASTLE, JR.

Charles was born in Maine in 1951. While his are roots deep in colonial New England, his heart has been planted in Oregon since 1978 where he worked in healthcare education and public affairs. He has published three books of poetry since retiring in 2014.

About these political poems:

"Given that we are all responsible for the state of affairs we find ourselves in, I like to include a historical context in my political rantings, and where that fails, rage into the surreal."

In this Land We've Taken

If schools don't teach the story
Of the road that we have run
Will our children feel the burden
Of the things that we have done
In this land that we have taken
With the ideals we profess
There's a brotherhood we've squandered
From a past we don't confess
Toward a setting sun we've traveled
Every day since we were born
In the morning light we've waited
For our country's heart to warm
In the courts of inquisition
Where they try the men of dreams
We have caught the tears of heaven
And worn them on our sleeves
As history repeats itself
When will the day begin
We're not plagued by our submission
And haunted by our sin
Where the church of endless war
Leaves its soldiers on a cross
The clergymen of conflict
Count their profit without cost
Where wars between religions
They manipulate for oil
Releasing deeper demons
While the holy water boils
We have gathered at black fountains
Watched the smoking derricks burn

And cast our prayers upon them
Is there anything we've learned
When they call the word of God
Like a curse upon the land
And mortgage every garden
For a fallow business plan
Is there really any reason
To expect a fertile spring
From those who call the season
By the market share it brings
When we will not feed the hungry
Or house them in their need
And we all are on their payroll
Where will the future lead
Can we prime the pump of giving
In the depth of all our hearts
To become the truly living
When our fears we let depart
Where hate is but a weapon
Fear uses to attack
War becomes the refuge
That rides upon its back
Is it endless in its marching
Off these cliffs we clearly see
Or can we nurture back to nature
Sustaining love we all set free

Of Armies and Generals

If flags were buried in lost graves
and from them bugles called no reveille
if the words of dead soldiers wrote history
and war held no memory past midnight's armistice
if conflict's profit was made bankrupt by honorable men
and weapons were re-forged into lasting community
then old generals could tend to armies of grandchildren
and perhaps a golden rule for peace could be negotiated
by widows and orphans
and only tears would become
memories

To the Ones Who Know

You can paint a coat of color
over all these things
You can get in bed with evil
and his seven kings
Or you can break a vow of silence
to command the wind
when Nero burns the cities
with his violin
When the scholars High and Holy
will stand no ground
and the voices in the choir
will sing no sound
someone paves the roadways
and draws the maps
that lead us to a wasteland
where they've set the traps
When the brown shirts wear the colors
of the red white and blue
And the people drink the Kool-Aid
what does freedom do
History repeats itself
but who reads books
and the ones that know ain't speakin'
when the rest are crooks
A cross with an agenda
wields a racist flame
A court rules for abuse
and it's a deadly game
If a dollar buys a sound-bite

that's believed as truth
freedom's just a slave
inside a voting booth

JEAN SHELDON

Creating art, poetry, and music has been a part of my life since childhood, but it wasn't until 2004, at the age of 53, that I began writing mysteries as a distraction to challenging political times. That was over 13 years ago, and although the challenges continue, writing has proven to be much more than a distraction. It has been a gift that taught me to look more closely and listen more attentively—to find answers beyond my limited view of the world. This, I hope, has made me a better person. It has instilled in me an optimism that a peaceful united humanity is possible.

The Weight of a Dream is a poem written during a creative dry spell. It became the outline for a collection of drawings and verse called *The Effects of Gravity on the Soul of a Poet*. Although never published, it was the spark that reignited my creative engine.

The Weight of a Dream

Dust settles
on my wings
and I shiver
in an unconscious
attempt to relieve it.
It remains
as if making
a point.
Weary from
the weight,
I become more
fixed to this earth,
less likely to fall,
haunted by dreams
of my failure to fly.
The soul of a poet
must travel beyond the
limits of gravity,
never trading
dreams for safety,
or wings for
firm ground.

MIKE SHULER

I am a retired educator and psychologist. I have published locally and regionally, edited my college literary magazine (Northwest Passage, Oregon College of Education, 1975), and am a North Carolina Poetry Society award winner. I was a featured reader at the 2015 Silverton Poetry Festival. I attend poetry events around the Salem area and participate in activity generated by the Mid-Valley Poetry Society.

"View from the Black Hills" represents a perspective experienced while visiting Mount Rushmore National Memorial and Crazy Horse Memorial in South Dakota. The poem illustrates my strong feelings about the ideals of America written and spoken but not lived, and also reflects the long-standing connection I have felt with Native America and the oppression of its people by the European immigrants who settled here.

View from the Black Hills

Outward over the vast rolling plain
Washington gazes into a future
Become present unlike that future
He envisioned for his beloved country
Jefferson looks down on his words
Defining freedom and justice for all
And fails to meet the eyes of the world
Roosevelt is distracted by another battle
He must fight for the destiny of man
And another trophy of bully strength
Lincoln sees the effects of civil struggle
Continuing to rip at the fabric of the flag
And seeks solace inward for his grief
While Crazy Horse rides the mountains
And Sioux lament the taking of land
And stand to defend an ancient claim

DENNIS WIEGAL

I am a life-long writer of poetry and music who lives with his wife of 47 years in Salem Oregon. We came to Oregon in 1976 to raise a family. I worked in the Chicago area as a clinical psychologist before moving west and working for the State of Oregon from which I am retired. I have two books of published poetry: "Progeny" (2015) and "Life in the Trenches" (2016).

"Politicians" pretty clearly shows my current view of the state of politics in America. I don't paint all politicians with this unattractive tint. But those who are to be painted using brighter hues are becoming the exception rather than the rule.

"Election Year 2016" was obviously written before Election Day. Had it been done following that day of infamy, there would have been less "dark humor" and simply more "darkness."

"The Dream" is a poem I wrote after I was able to recover from my stupor over the election results. It reflects my love for America and belief in our people's goodness and strength through the darkest of nights.

Election Year 2016

the final episode of our reality show careens closer
with terrifying speed ripe with unthinkable possibilities
unscripted insanity feeds the flames which ignited
by foolish sparks at the start of the season became an inferno
that devours reason here at season's end
Hail to the Chief has been erased replaced
by the theme from Looney Tunes
Will Porky or Elmer at least explain it
to Bugs and me answer that essential question:
What's Up Doc? What's Up Doc?
how did our choices become limited
to the Tasmanian Devil tweeting his need for walls
and Road Runner vying to outdistance and outspend
Wile E. Coyote who brandishes his Acme
Socialism Users' Guide before fascinated and fearful eyes
still we had a good run these past 240 years
now as the cancellation date nears
the cartoon characters cry out louder and louder
the closing line to end our program:
th-th-th-that's all folks

Politicians

the question echoed from the audience:
why do you blather on so,
rigid, clenched,
shut to anything
that does not ring in resonance
with the overflowing chamber pots
that crowd your mind?
the politician continued without pause
filling the air with a most fetid aroma

The Dream

so many good men so many good women
almost invisible mute and still
where are they now when needed the most
in this time which tests our courage and will
why aren't their voices overpowering the haters
and empowering dreamers who still cling to the dream
the dream of a people united in honor
one people from many who want to believe
in a welcoming land without walls
regardless of color gender or creed
a land where life is cherished by all
a land where love can still win over greed
does that seem silly is that naïve
a mere child's fantasy best dead to the mind?
is it more grown-up to no longer believe
in this place of promise to leave it behind?
our fathers and mothers paid a high price
for that which we now see withering away
is their hunger for a brighter tomorrow forgotten
no longer felt by the people today
so many good men so many good women
how to rekindle passion grown cold
time for one dreamer to speak out with courage
time for the dream to again take hold

ELEANOR BERRY

As long as I can remember, I've identified with individuals and groups maligned by more powerful individuals and groups, and I've wanted to give those misrepresented and mistreated strength by expressing their perspective in my writing. At the same time, I've been skeptical of my ability to enter fully into any perspective except my own, and fearful that I would inadvertently violate those whose lives I meant to give voice. Thus, though I love reading persona poems, I rarely write them. Instead, as in the poems here, I try to imagine the experience of others while also making clear that my imagination is limited by the actual scope of my own experience.

I grew up in southern Connecticut, an only child with a love for wild plants and animals and for books. Since then, with my husband, astronomy writer and photographer, Richard Berry, I've come slowly west. We lived in Ontario, Canada, where I received my Ph. D. from the University of Toronto, and then Wisconsin before moving to western Oregon in 1994. Here, we settled in rural Lyons, where we have a tiny herd of alpacas and a small observatory. Our home makes an ideal writing retreat.

During my first few years in Oregon, I taught writing and literature at Willamette University, as I had done earlier at Marquette University and other colleges in Wisconsin. While I've written poetry since childhood and published it since early in graduate school, it didn't become my primary focus until I left university teaching in 1999. Over the years, my poems have been published in numerous literary magazines and anthologies and collected in two books, Green November and No Constant Hues, both published by Oregon independent presses.

Questions No One Asks Me

Are you American?
Where do you come from?
What are you doing here?
Why don't you go back home?
No one thinks to ask me
because I'm fair-skinned
and speak standardAmerican English.
So I'm American—right?
It dependson what is meant
by *American*.
I've lived all my life
in America—
on this continent called
North America.
Born in New York City,
I'm a naturalized Canadian citizen
now living in the United States
as a *resident alien*.
Where do I come from?
It depends
on what is meant
by *from*. I came
here to the Pacific Northwest
from the Great Lakes—or
from Connecticut by way
of Pennsylvania, Virginia, Ontario,
and Wisconsin.
I came to the United States

from Canada, went to Canada
from the United States.
What am I doing here
in western Oregon?
On a plot of rocky land, once
riverbed, now pasture and woods,
I'm living with my husband,
the creatures we care for,
and the sundry wild ones
that dwell or forage around us.
Why don't I go back home?
Every place I've lived
I've made my home.
Now my home is here.
But if my skin were not
what is called *fair*,
if I spoke with a foreign
accent or in a so-called
non-standard dialect,
would I have been able—
even in so long a time
and with so great an effort
as it has taken me—
to feel at home here?
That's a question
I can't answer.

Swallow Song

Philomela, virgin raped by her sister's
rich and powerful husband, Tereus, who then
cut out her tongue and locked her up,
found a way to tell her sorrow, his crime.
She wove it all, so Ovid recounts,
into a tapestry, and escaped Tereus' pursuit
by changing from her human form
into a bird, took wing as a swallow.
There is no sorrow like the murmur of their wings
The pressed millions wronged by America's
rich and powerful president, Trump, who now
has gagged and banned them, ordered them out,
will find a way to sing, a way to fly.
There is no choir like their song
There is no power like the freedom of their flight

> *Italicized lines are from "The Swallow Song,"*
> *by Joan Baez.*

What We Call It

Rendition we call it when a painter
depicts a place or face
with brushstrokes laid
on paper, wood, or canvas;
when an orchestra
performs a score;
a theater troupe
puts on a play;
when a storyteller gives an old tale
a new slant; or a translator
carries over a text
into a new language.
Extraordinary rendition we call it
when a prisoner is delivered
to a jurisdiction where
torture is common practice.
To render a scene, a story, a song
is to take it and change it—
to wrest it into
a different form.
In the most perfect likeness,
the most faithful translation,
something
has been violated:
The subject has surrendered
to the artist's will.
The source has been
overwritten.

Pen, brush, baton
do lethal swordplay.
To render is to melt down.
To rend is to tear apart.

JM.PERSÁNCH

JM.Persánch is a professor, literary, film and cultural critic, editor and writer. He appreciates creative forms as a path to both exploring human nature and better understanding contemporary societies. Since 2006, he has routinely published scholarly papers, poetry, and short-stories. He edited four collections of poems as founding director of the Palabras Indiscretas literary group. He has been the managing editor of several academic and literary journals in Spain and the U.S. He is currently immersed in various projects comprising poetry, micro-fiction, and prose-fiction novel.

In "The Wall", JM.Persánch expresses his concern about the rise of intolerance, the naturalization of xenophobia and the justification of racism which the wall in the Southern border symbolizes. "The Wall" revisits Mexican History to write a counter-discourse that speaks up against the overt criminalization of Mexicans as well as the stigmatization of both Latino culture and newcomers in the US. In sum, the author cries against the dangers of exercising a political and social amnesia that could condemn us to repeat a History of the worst kind. For further information and contact http://jmpersanch.com.

The Wall

(To Mexican immigrants, to all immigrants.)

I am going to build a Wall:
A beautiful, tall, thick as hell,
huge as well, unbreakable wall...
And Mexico is going to pay for it.
[...]

Hey!
Look at them, they exist:
They are the great wall,
framed by the hatred of your executive pen,
detained in your tower of dreadful amnesia,
the puppets of your sadistic political game,
mere scapegoats whose bodies, once again,
become an American battleground,
where enemies are brown clowns
painted hanging in the clouds.
But they are the wall that will endure
because, understand this,
they are the wall of time!
You seed fear, like Cortés did for 300 years,
you want them to have
at home: no home and no hope,
and abroad: no hope and no home.
You spit horror,
here and there.
But they'll resist
carrying generosity on their backs!
(Though it is sad, not knowing which side to turn or run to).

They are the wall that deflects your greed.
They, too, aim at you... with empty stomachs nonetheless.
       They are you, unborn. They are them, reborn.
Their sweat, blood and tears made and make America great,
       And they are here to stay.
          THEY EXIST.

C. STEVEN BLUE

Steven C. Schreiner (C. Steven Blue)

Poet/publisher, multimedia performance artist, producer/host of poetry events, including a monthly reading series at Barnes & Noble, Eugene, Oregon. Steven has six published books; has published other poets and anthologies for the city of Eugene and the Oregon Poetry Association; has been published in 12 countries, interviewed on television, radio and in literary magazines; has performed from coast to coast. His work appears in numerous literary journals and anthologies, in print and online. More information can be found on his website www.wordsongs.com.

In thinking about my three poems, all of them were directly influenced by the 2016 Presidential Election. All three poems poured right out of me. I was not attempting to write or doing any writing discipline, they each just poured out quickly, all influenced by what was exploding, politically, all around us at the time.

(hashtag) Not My President was written the day after the election, November 9, 2016

Delerium Clouds and The End were written in February 2017, on a road trip from Eugene to Sacramento, CA to help my 95 year old father. Delerium Clouds was written in my car on the trip down while listening to the music of Delerium and The End was written in my car on the trip back, almost a week later. The election and politics were still very much on my mind and a strong influence in both of these pieces of work.

(hashtag) Not My President

I was there that night . . .
the night when Democracy fell.
I was there when hate trumped love
and I don't know what will happen now.
I see a dark mist rising,
a chilled wind is in the air.
I don't know where we stand
         going forward,
but I know that hope is still there.
So hate and oppression
have won out over love and compassion
for just this little while,
but we will never accept that, Mr. Trump,
no matter how much you sniffle and smile.
You are not my President,
nor will you ever be.
I will never approve of racism and hate
. . . or misogyny.
I will never be in collusion
with Russia, our greatest enemy.
They would take us over in a heartbeat
from sea to shining sea.
As long as there are freedom fighters,
we will look you in the eye
and say . . .
"A dictator may control your destiny,
but this will never be our way!"
Hatred, racism and misogyny
have no place in our land.

As long as America has been here
the good-hearted have always taken a stand.
You may try to quell our voices
and drive us to despair,
but we always rise up again
stronger,
to make the rest of you aware
that freedom means responsibility,
for those less fortunate than you.
The rich and the greedy
think they control it all,
but this will never do.
So you must rise up
for what you believe in.
Never bow down to the gun
that kills you and your children
with poverty and sickness,
tries to keep you in fear
and on the run.
I have fought this battle
for over 50 years,
but now it is time for the young
to take up the struggle of equality.
We have only just begun!
I hope they do a better job then we did
to bring it out into the light,
that bigotry and hatred will not be tolerated,
for equality is our right.
I was there that night . . .
the night when Democracy fell.
I was there when hate trumped love

and I don't know what will happen now.
But he is not my President,
nor will he ever be.
I will never approve of racism and hate
. . . or misogyny.

Delerium Clouds

I saw the hope of my generation
strangled and crushed
by greed and lust
—for power.
Compassion for our fellow man
seems vanquished in a day,
by the un-attended sorrow
of the smashing of tomorrow,
of the anger and the shame
that remain.
Like three Mustangs and a Porsche
roaring down the highway,
snow-capped mountains
crumbling at their side.
Can't go fast enough
to chase it away,
this feeling of loss
and the rapid decay
of what took so long to build,
of what cannot be remade
. . . in a day,
of the struggle, the pain
and the heartache
coming our way.
Driving through *Delerium* clouds,
growing darker every day.
Is it true that hope is fading;
shadow walls and decay?
Can you see the flames of madness,
      filled with sadness,

    filled with grief?
Can you tell me
what will happen;
give me some relief?
Spin it now
—fake the mourning,
Kingdoms come
and feigned divine!
Take it to the 7th wonder
in another time.
Calling, calling, calling now.
Crawling, crawling, crawling now.
Falling, falling, falling
til we're done.
Climb up to the curbside,
climb up to the dirt.
It's all gone
. . . And nobody has won!
Three Mustangs and a Porsche
roaring down the highway,
snow-capped mountains
crumble at their side.
Can't go fast enough
to chase it away,
this feeling of loss
and the rapid decay
of what took so long to build,
of what cannot be remade
. . . in a day,
of the struggle, the pain

and the heartache
coming our way.

The End

Brown sweeping fingers
of delinear repose;
reaching, clutching...blurry browns,
perched against the cloudy remains
of dripping skies.
Vast green rivers
of melancholy grass.
Grouping birds...swooping by;
hundreds and hundreds
swiping the sky
directly in front of our eyes.
Tractor traces
gobbling up the linear spaces,
divided by the human races
voting to be heard.
Folded up machinery
waiting to be found;
awaits to be sound again
and billowing clouds of dust,
if you must...know.
You've been beating back the storm,
but now it is upon you
and it's not turning back.
It is raining, it is pouring;
quickly picking up the slack
until it is upon you
and beats you to the ground;
your arrogance

never to be found again.
It is the end!
Armies of trees,
barren to the bone,
have been your legacy;
captured currents
of unrighteous cause,
sworn to secrecy.
Creeping up the banks
of sorrow,
haystacks hover
until they dry.
Dead wood stacked up
by the roadside
never made you sigh,
but warms us. . . by and by
until we die.
In the blink of an eye
you blew it,
tore it to the core!
Ignorance—
and blinding madness
always end in war.
Putting it back together, though,
will surely take some time.
It always is a HEAVY struggle,
coming back from the BLIND!!!

DR. VERONICA ESAGUI

Dr. Veronica Esagui, is a chiropractic physician, and the internationally and critically acclaimed author of the Scoliosis Self-Help Resource Book (English and Japanese) and Veronica's Diary series. She specializes in public speaking, and is the founder of "The Authors Forum," (TV talk show) and The Northwest Writers and Publishers Association, and NW Annual Book Festival (2008–2015).

The Ghost of the Future

She did not feel her existence among the living
no one saw her
not in the familiar streets
and much less when she entered the cemetery.
She looked for them
They would remember her.
They lived in her mind, in her deepest thoughts.
They were alive when she last saw them
then she saw the stones lying next to each other.
Where was hers?
She was the ghost of the future
There was no middle
And there was no beginning.

Make America Great Again?

Trumpetti tramp, trump tramp, there he goes along with the rest
Not to be confused with the best.
Those who voted for Trumpetti Tramp, trump tramp
Wanted something new, nothing more and nothing less.
Now we have more of nothing and less of something
Not to be confused with anything that matters because he is
the president and what he says
doesn't have to be true or make any sense.

SAMANTHA LINDSEY

Samantha is a registered Independent in the state of Oregon. The incomplete sestina was inspired by relentless professor, peer, media, and social media gibing. This poem is evidence. There was a girl in a blue state, who welcomed all sides and ultimately voted red.

Unaccounted

A sestina, the United States of America. May 3, 2017
Monmouth, Oregon
Western Oregon University
Business Office Assistant's Desk
The sound of Taylor Swift's album *Red* knocks on my ears;
my hand darts for the iPhone 4, ancient and worn.
The little black block stares back at a third-year-college-student,
judging as one swipe soothes my friend back to silence.
The cotton in/of my pillow is not abandoned
until I click on Yahoo news.
My tired eyes would shoot open, at the latest news.
Instead they roll at the headline, and still, I open my ears.
The art of fact collecting and compilation has been abandoned;
and journalists explicitly vomit content: and their best-guessed bias
delivered. Worn—attempts to excite do no justice to empty wordy-
pages that leave real thought in silence. Catchy, cat-fishing titles deliver
the message transparently; whom deserves judging?
No questions. Sit, type, pay tuition, and listen. A literature professor
taunts. Mocking him, judging.
Jokes regurgitated from the *Daily Show with Trevor Noah,* and more
follow, at the expense of Fox News. Classroom laughter roars, and
internal commentary binds my fingers tightly to my keyboard: silence.
And ears
scream—hoisting hashtag splattered signs endorsed by Huffington Post
Op-Eds—and cat ears are worn
by fellow citizens, while notions of independent thought are
abandoned.
Isolated in a universe of like-thought, I sit, abandoned
by the promise of university for objective analyses without exception.
But, simpler is judging,

and colorful apps for selfies with playful filters are much more pleasing than the worn

permanent aroma of exhaustion and bitterness, caused by the pretentious rape of truth from news,

and by journalists spoonfeeding *the* agenda to an audience without ears:

grown toddlers tantrum for another dollop of strawberry yogurt, and appeasement is the chosen method for silence.

My eyes keep ahead of the words as they appear on my glowing white screen—just cymbals to unravel the silence; *You don't count. You don't count.* Give a second thought, ask a single question, or don't. Don't.

Or be abandoned by the social fraternity you never asked to be sworn into. And Forche's peach-half ears

burn my eyes as the brothers and sisters line up to pay dues. The next tilts her head upward for judging,

and cartilage pinched by an authoritative hand is stripped from her, and proudly she poses for the school news—with a rag pressed against the right of her face. I've kept my hearing, yet she carries a smile I've never worn.

And so I look hard at the bathroom mirror, every morning, checking the purple, pale bags worn

beneath green irises. Splashing ice water against the wrinkles of my skin in silence,

brushing the makeup powder on, a hot mug of coffee rests at my side. I reach and point, channel 360, Fox News—and *some* relief is reached at the sight of some two-eared representatives: a demographic largely abandoned

by a slanted media, with a contemporary mission consisting of assuming, judging;

a quiet breath escapes as my fingers reach for each lobe of my ears.

Alternating soles scrape against the university sidewalk; and I've become accustomed to the quiet. Abandoned, for ears—for lobes which *bleed the red blood of patriots—*
one unaccounted vote: a young woman, still with both ears.

NANCY CHRISTOPHERSON

I wrote each of these poems within the first quarter of 2017 after the November 2016 election, when I felt compelled to write socially-engaged, politically-edged poems as a sort of cathartic antidote against the chaos. I wanted to lend a voice to those without a voice, to offer hope. To say, here, look, all is not lost but it could be.

Nancy Christopherson, author of "The Leaf" (2015), has work published or forthcoming in "Hawai'i Pacific Review," "Helen," "Peregrine," "Raven Chronicles," "Third Wednesday," "Verseweavers," "Willawaw Journal," "Xanadu," and the anthology "Weaving the Terrain: 100-Word Southwestern Poems" from Dos Gatos Press. Currently immersed in found full-length manuscripts-in-progress, she lives and writes in eastern Oregon.

Visit www.nancychristophersonpoetry.com.

Water as Much as Anything

When everything else fails—that is,
humanity—this sparse, spilling, H20
enlivens the living, the still-living tissues.
A catbird calls from its tree in Nevada,
does not stop searching for mates nor
protection of habitat. Sings: Water! Water!
Come. Sip. That we may continue. Not
words enough, not the small quizzical notes,
but the full-throated rapturous bell-tones. From
the heights of the catbird's perch in the green
aspen these truths fall. Not one human in sight.

Migrants Immigrants Welcome

Forgive our ignorance, not everyone is
stupid or cruel. Your ancient tongues,
sacred texts are equal to any culture.
Nothing excludes like lack of understanding.
Welcome, please, come back, keep trying.
Let these words stand for something
bigger than a red baseball cap. Our ears have
been plugged with infection, our eyes
blinded by rage. One man does not
have exclusive permission. Fences do not
contain anyone. May we build on that.
May we learn new expressions together.

Greater Good

Kiss the hearts
on my jogging shorts when I lift them
from the dryer, sniff
the dryer sheets.
When I lean over to change
the linens of your bed
reach down your hands to help
tuck in the corners. It is back-
breaking work. The sun
shines in through some curtains
and a breeze lifts them.
There are chickadees, finches,
plus cardinals to brighten
the branches.
Let us take caution—not to
disappear in the dim light of
exclusion. No vines
grow there, no succulent
fruit.
No water hits ground.
Gather one pebble. Keep gathering.
These are very dark times.

At the Human Test Site

Every other frame
in this scenario is authentic.
Those in between
are falsehoods—
these are not marked
for you—you
will not know which
is which until later—
at the end, or after.
Try not to choose which is
which for you. There is no
correct answer—they are
all incorrect. So,
quick, pick your
poison. Take your weapon,
lay it down.

MARILYN JOHNSTON

After the election, writing served as the salve to soothe the pain that I felt, along with so many others, in our community. I wrote to make sense of those first days. This poem grew out of that initial frustration, which quickly mobilized into collective action, and finally, unmitigated hope—bringing comfort in the sound.

With One Voice

I sit in a room of strong men and women
and it's like a therapy group.
The ones who still talk about sleepless nights,
the tears that won't stop, still incredulous—
the fears, the divisions, the sheer lunacy,
the new President's irrational words
about our country being in a mess, a mess.
The real fake news.
It's as if the world around us has gone mad,
and we're still in that hazy shock upon first
awakening from a dreamless state after a fever.
I can't shake it, this foreboding.
Can't rationalize it away by reading
Facebook and Twitter—
although the first week, these seemed
like a lifeline.
The mere act of making signs together
the day before the Women's March—
like art therapy for the drowning.
I got to the Salem Capitol grounds early.
The day's cold rain echoed our discomfort.
There is solidarity in fear, the determined arms
linked with strangers who suddenly become
like the family we didn't recognize.
So many of us, young and old, dancing,
as we spilled out through the Salem streets—
hands raised, voices united, in something
that resembled resistance, some belief
that the world will survive this,

leaving us buoyed, resolute.
A pledge that will take us into the streets
each day, singing out loud.

LISA E. BALDWIN

Lisa E. Baldwin is a writer, teacher and farmer who believes poetry is necessary for a good life. A fifth-generation Oregon native, her poetry draws on the beauty, diversity and history of our place. She lives on a little farm in the Lower Applegate Valley with her husband and honeybees. Baldwin works with two groups of fellow Southern Oregon poets, The Applegate Poets and the Pagan Warrior Poets. She is also a member of the Oregon Poetry Association, currently serving as OPA's president and co-chair of the Cascadia Contest for Oregon's K-12 students.

For Emma Lazarus

True to her name, may she rise
Renewed and come to be
Known by new generations
Of tired, poor, huddled and homeless
Invited by this mighty woman
Whose words still lead and light our way.
Deaf men, pompous and wretched,
Forge old metal, recast the mission
And dead-bolt the doors that used to swing free.
Legions of women, persistent and teeming,
Cut new keys, bridge old divides
And work together to keep doors open,
To welcome our neighbors,
To care for our wounded,
To feed all our children kindness and hope,
And uphold the creed of decent people.
Women awakened carry the lightning torch,
Shine liberty's light into the dark cells
Where corruption spreads like black mold.
Women together, voices raised, hackles up
Drive the devils down on their soft knees,
Unused to bending for any, certainly not these
Women—around the world, across the divide, next door—
Rise up! Rise up!
Our time is now.

Lazarus Sunday in Tanta

Here where understanding God
Overbears all else, and where the same
Historical facts were long ago transfigured
Into three intransigent myths, cemented
By countless wars of men
Crazed by dreams of personal glory.
They prove countless times there is
No God of Love to raise another Lazarus.
So sweep up the shards of broken oaths.
Lay down unsalted palms.
The clamored air is perfumed with blood
And the trees have withered, all.

Letter to the Other Humans on Planet Earth

Dear Neighbors,
We can do it better.
We can take these apples, fresh and whole
To that old playground behind
The shuttered cabinet mill. Children there
Might be made to smile
By our outstretched hands
Bearing the gift of these apples.
They are hungry there
Where hardships grow and apples do not.
We can do it better.
We can grow our understanding of kinship
So the practice of Family spreads and flows freely,
Beyond our veins and borders
To enfold our Brothers and Sisters,
Embrace our common humanity.
All People of the World:
Spill no more blood, cut no more ties.
We can heal the divisions that sever us.
We can do it better.
We can love the planet whole again,
Air and Water, Earth and Sky.
Wrap the children in soft quilts,
Let them drink safe water, breathe clean air,
Know the light of Home,
Harvest from the Earth, let them
Dream of flying with the birds above,
Eat fresh apples and love.

LAURENCE OVERMIRE

Laurence Overmire is a poet, author, actor, director, educator and genealogist from West Linn, Oregon. "Much of my work comes out of two simple ideas," he says. "The first is The Golden Rule: Do unto others as you would have them do unto you. And the second is We are One. All of us are one family, interconnected and interdependent upon one another for our well being. And central to both of these ideas are love and compassion. So a lot of what I write about are the things I see in the world that somehow violate these two ideas. I am deeply concerned about what I see happening in the United States as the divisions and tensions among our citizens become more and more extreme." For more about the author, go to laurenceovermire.com.

I woke up one morning

I woke up one morning
In a country I didn't know
I was a stranger, a foreigner
And I had no right to be
Who I was
I was lost
And alone
And I wandered through the reasoning
Of why men do the things they do
And I couldn't find any answers
I kept tripping over barbed-wire hate
Cutting into the color of my skin and the
Fragility of my once fervently held
Beliefs
Of what the world was all about
I came to question
Everything
There was nothing sacred
In the meanness of spirit
That corrodes the unenlightened
Tin-panned heart yearning
For some travesty of
Salvation
Bleeding, but undeterred
I crossed over
Into another realm
Of being
I am who I am now
I have awakened

They will not take me away from me
No matter what they do
To stop the human spirit
From its inevitable climb to
Redemption
The haters will be overcome
They always have
They always will
The truth is bigger than any of us
Will ever know or see
Let go of fear
It is an illusion and a lie
Hang on to love
It will always lead you where you
Wish you were and ultimately
Need
To be.

One Wrong Choice

May make the difference
There are people you will find
In the crossroads of your life
To be toxic
They are the bringers down
The manipulators
The destroyers
That are never to be trusted
They will lead you
To the worst in yourself and others
Never the best
Their very presence
Hovers over the world
Like an impending doom
A nightmare calamity
About to be
Unleashed
Avoid them
Steer clear
Defend
You must protect
The safe place
Within yourself
The holy and sacred space
Bequeathed to you
In the very beginning
Of all that is good
The noble and steadfast truth
That keeps the horrors of the
Darkening world

At bay.

The Neighbor Next Door

Seems to be a nice person
But
He believes a lot of things he sees
On the Internet
He believes things that have no basis
In fact
He trusts people whose hearts are filled
With hate
And sometimes his eyes flare with
Vengeance
He can't understand why we won't see
His truth
We are at a loss—and so is he
How can you reason with unreasonable
People?
This is the hopelessness of our
Divide
In America's 21st century
And it's frightening.

JOY MCDOWELL

In this poem I juxtapose mankind's failures with a yearned-for-god to fix environmental problems. In truth, humanity must step forward and repair what we have broken. There is no magic shortcut. Greed has a price and future generations will pay the price in suffering.

I have spent my life watching birds, climbing mountains and trusting the lessons I see in nature. The natural world has the ability to heal people, but not always heal itself. The fate of mankind and nature are sealed together.

I write from both the Willamette Valley and the Coos Bay estuary. The back and forth pattern of tidal flow assists me in finding new energy and fresh beginnings in a sometimes bleak world. Turkey vultures are one of my favorite species of birds. They always come to clean up the aftermath of a glorious life and an inevitable struggle.

At The Zoo

With muddy thread a kind god
would stitch the plates of the planet
back together, would anchor glaciers
in their cold place, put a stitch in the hole
of the ozone layer. Instead, greedy humans
soil their orb and fail to patch what we ruin.
The smartest and most clever of species
maps out small repair plans and argues
over money and labor, even
elects a climate change denier.
A kind god would teach her minions
to share food and water, the nurturing
paste of community and globe. Warriors
of many nations would attack disease,
the suffering of man and beast. Instead,
the blue marble and her fractious zoo
of Ripley's inhabitants
circles the cosmic clock like
a dog chasing its tail.

A. ROZ MAR

A. Roz Mar is an author of fiction, non-fiction philosophy and screenplays, and a veil painting artist. For many years she has been in private practice as a psychotherapist. She is a Doctor of Philosophy in Esoteric Religious Studies; "Politics is not separate from our daily lives. The threefold nature of nations is made up of a cultural society, economics and politics. We must see them as a totality so to understand that all three exist at the core of human beings progress, at any given moment, in an ever evolving history."

A. Roz Mar http://www.bluepearlarts.com

Tweetelection

Voices, opinions and insights fill the airways, Flashes of cameras,
News clicks away rapidly into the cloud.
A race, an election
Like "no other" a daily affair.
Tweetle Dumb Tweetle Dee
Rumors, hysterics, lies and deceit, "No other like it,"
Twenty sixteen
Campaign promises to be a good one. "If he wins, I'll leave the
country," "If she wins I'll send her to jail."
Lost footage, an outrage,
Lights out, he'll call it quits "Impossible! It cannot be, groping for
popularity." Red and Blue faces leer
Into the negative lights of the camera Alternative facts
That do not lie down easily.
Tweetle Dumb Tweetle Dee
Despot, crackpot,
Email witch hunt, Protracted evidence, Her time in office, A secretary
of state Bemoan the affront. Make your vote count!
One-a-penny,
Two-a-penny Three-a-penny four
Tax evasion
A million to one What's another million more, More billionaires than
before
Flattery, flattery, flattery Flynn
Respite please,
Turn off your cell phone while the newsreel rolls, As not once but
twice
The emperor, all a-twitter, wears no clothes. Watch Mar-a-Lago
Fall into the Bay of Biscayne Meanwhile a Washington hurricane
"Let's blame the wasteful EPA!"

Tweetle Dumb Tweetle Dee
Mark the four year calendar. When will it end? Early is better
Late than never Impeachable offence
A Russian defense of De facto friends
Tweetle Dumb
Tweetle Dee,
Twittter tweet a short term memory. Facebook pals discuss and abhor,
Clean up the social media mess On your way out the door.

ROSALYN KLIOT

Rosalyn Kliot is an award winning and published artist currently residing in the Pacific Northwest. Born in Eastern Europe, she resided in Poland, Germany, and finally, she arrived in America on her 2nd birthday. She is a retired Vocational Rehabilitation Counselor, an occupation she held for 30 years.

Rosalyn studied art, first at the University of Illinois, Navy Pier, in Chicago, and then Roosevelt University where she completed her BA in Art on a full scholarship.

Her work has been juried into numerous shows and galleries and has been exhibited and sold in Chicago, Los Angeles, Oregon, Washington. She also has work in a traveling show in Tokyo, Japan, as well as well as in private and corporate collections.

She is author of a memoir "My Father's Book," which is archived at the US Holocaust Museum in Washington, DC.

"I wrote the poem in response to the current political atmosphere, where, almost daily, the nation is bombarded with misinformation, half truths and outright lies, disseminated by the administration...it has frequently seemed to me that I am living in an altered state of reality...what is real...what is true?"

All Things Considered

Consider what seems real in your life,
Is it memory of a past long gone,
Or events not yet done,
Or a dream floating on air or drifting in wind
And dissolving in dust...?
Ponder on thoughts as beliefs.
Are they rock hard solid and dark
Or deep with Light and Joy,
Fire red heat enflamed,
Or waves of a cool emerald blue?
Consider all things as they are.
And inhale the meaning of Truth,
Ephemeral and illusive they are
Like gossamer blurring the seen.
Silence remains to be heard.

SUSAN PATTERSON

Susan Patterson is an unexpected author. She did not put writing into her life's plan. However, after a demanding and busy career in business and upon retirement, much to her surprise, poetry began coming to her. Ms. Patterson is an author of the heart and writer for the soul. Her work, it has been said, is so sharp, so intricate, that it is like a Faberge egg. Ms. Patterson's audience is worldwide and declares her writing to be in the top caliber of modern poets. Her work, which ranges from humorous to thoughtfully intelligent is always quietly compelling.

Not A Total Loss

Each of us has the ability
To help Humanity grow.
This is true because
Every once in a while
We do things right.
Every once in a while
We take in a stray.
Love the wretched.
Care for the weak.
Give a little grace.
Every once in awhile,
We bend a bit lower
To raise the bar
Just a little higher.
Every once in awhile,
We get things right.

The Cry of the Obvious

I am just one voice
Crying for humanity
Raging in the world of
Anger and pain and violence.
There are many more voices,
Louder than mine,
Who come from wealth and power,
Who will tell you
That the way we live is right.
I am just one voice,
Crying for humanity,
Saying, it is not.

PENELOPE SCHOTT

Penelope Scambly Schott is a past recipient of the Oregon Book Award for Poetry. Her newest books are Serpent Love: A Mother-Daughter Epic, an exploration of a crisis between mother and adult daughter, and a collection called Bailing the River. She lives in Portland and Dufur, Oregon where she teaches an annual poetry workshop. www.penelopescamblyschott.com. Her innate sense of reason and decency is violated every day by our current president.

"The First Three Weeks of the First Hundred Days" coincided with destructive storms and landslides in Portland, adding to the general sense of catastrophe.

"No Use at All" reflects the overwhelmed hopelessness of a generally optimistic person.

In "Report from India" I attempt to describe how what was a quick, lost story in the United States was a major tragedy in India. In my time in India, I have met many young tech workers hoping to get visas to work in the United States. Here is how hope ended for one such young man.

No Use at All

No use sending money to feed the Somali kid
with the standard sunken cheeks and bloated belly
He and his brothers will have rough lives
and be killed in some local war that makes
the New York Times
No use wrapping a quilt around the woman
asleep in a doorway in the winter rain
She will get soaked anyhow and die
of pneumonia
No reason to give up your seat
to the tottery old man on the number 20 bus
He will trip getting off that bus and never
walk again
No point in saying You, too
when the check-out girl wishes you a nice day
Her day will be long and underpaid and her feet
will go numb in her thrift store shoes and when
the shift finally ends and she makes it home
her kids will be bored and angry and won't
have started their homework
No use writing this shit down
and you know it and you know it and you know it
but there's this foolish little part of your mind
that comes strolling into your dry house
and can almost pretend that your dog
who stretches and yawns on the couch cushions
is mouthing *I love you too*

Report from India

*—in memory of Srinivas Kuchibhotla, age 32,
killed in a Kansas bar, February 2, 2017*

It's in all their English-language headlines,
the young married tech worker from India
out for an evening with friends,
killed in a bar in Kansas.
Also in the Hindi headlines
and the Malayalam headlines
and the Gujarati headlines
and all those curly alphabets I can't read.
Inside the green Periyar Tiger Preserve
the invisible tigers are talking,
and the visible monkeys,
and the long-tailed Malabar squirrels,
and the rocket-tailed drongo bird,
screaming. They talk about my country.
They are discussing my fellow citizens,
they are screaming my shame.
When I fly back to America
everyone has already forgotten,
everyone but the young man's wife
who will fly home to India
and open the sandalwood chest
containing her gold-embroidered wedding sari,
her stacked red wedding bracelets, dangling
earrings and necklace, the glittering set.

The First Three Weeks of the First Hundred Days

This is a factual fact.
Day by day, it keeps on coming.
Rain. Hail. The winds
that brought branches crashing down.
Three of darkness.
Three days of cold.
A lighter rain. Flakes
floating. Once
a snippet of blue sky.
But if you weren't looking,
you missed it.
Another executive order.
New snow on top of dirty snow.
Ice.
It was the ice that was the worst,
paws of the old dog
splaying in a four directions.
She looked at me
with baffled accusation.
More and heavier rain.
The saturated hillsides
slipping down the hillsides
Darlings, where are we going?

TIM RAPHAEL

I wrote On Patience to try to make sense of things after reading the following paragraph in the New York Times on April 13, 2017:

"The United States dropped the 'mother of all bombs'—the most powerful conventional bomb in the American arsenal—on an Islamic State cave complex in Afghanistan on Thursday, the Pentagon said, unleashing a weapon so massive that it had to be dropped from the rear of a cargo plane."

Tim Raphael lives with his family in Portland's Mt. Tabor neighborhood. He writes early each morning before heading to work at Strategies 360 where he provides communications advice to non-profit and business clients.

On Patience

Patience is knowing there was water here once
and very well could be again.
Like having a clock, geared to eons, with a face
large as a desert. No second hand needed when rivers cut rock.
My clock runs fast, chasing patience away. I *try*
as if effort is what patience demands.
And marvel at the ones who have figured out that with patience
it is never too late.
You know who I mean. Yogis, for sure, but also gardeners and bakers
and piano teachers who manage not to twitch with each clanked note,
ranchers sweaty from digging post-holes, their untroubled scent
calming the herd, and birders who know how to barely move.
And readers who read, not we who skim headlines
between sips of caffeine, tssking the latest outrage and scandal.
Still, the wisdom of patience confounds these days
when the forecast seems to call for alarm.
Do you see what I see when I take account?
We just dropped the Mother of All Bombs after all.
What does the gardener do now, I wonder?
Abandon the plot? Call in the weeds?
No. He gardens of course, because there's nothing new in atrocity,
and that was not the only thing to happen this week.
There was the afternoon I stood still for a moment
in a downpour so drenching I saw tulips give in,
shedding petals like life rafts of yellow and pink.

ARIEL

Pacific Northwest poet Ariel, is a professional poet & writer. She has been most recently published in MVPA's Write The Town chapbook & PlatChals's Travel; past publishing include traditional periodicals, anthologies and her official website poetariel.net. An advocate for "Think Globally, Act Locally," Ariel often collaborates in local poetry/art projects such as Speaking Peace, Salem Peace Mural Project & Visual-Verbal events. She is a member of several poetry organizations including Mid-Valley Poetry Association (WVPA), Oregon State Poetry Association (OPA), and Willamette Writers.

Ariel is known for her confessional Plathian works and her sublime erotica—seldom writing about the world of politics, even though she avidly follows and participates in current issues. But then Nov 16th happened...and the poem natural poured out. And every day since then, her pen writes globally—a voice added to those demanding our world not slide back into hate, ignorance and inhumanity.

containment: This poem kept getting louder in my head—as the current administration's demand for a border wall kept getting louder. And as the call for a wall got louder, so did the calls for bullying cruelty. Like many citizens, I have become so ashamed of what our country is becoming and I am afraid of what we may become—if not stopped.

in a cereal box: There is a loud voice in the United States that insists that known proven knowledge is made-up fairy-tales and that illogical, cobbled together esoterica is God's Endorsed Truth. I have watched the growing strength of the glorification of ignorance and hate, being fed through the new administration as something healthy and needed for our nation...like a cereal box of fake food.

natural: I'm sure I'm not the only one who felt, waking up Nov 9th, that the world had slid into some Orwellian fable; everything that felt solid and real the day before felt contrived and as unsubstantial as a thin sheet of paper. Hate had won out. Friends who feared becoming second-hand citizens were now having it become their reality. One of my favorite poets started trying to develop an exit plan, as her husband was a Muslim who renounced his homeland—where was there a safe place in the world?

In addition, I should note that these poems were written in a lower case structure—not so much as an homage to ee cummings - more as a reflection that everything these days is being diminished, losing it's inherent importance. This change in my writing developed in early 2016, and is integral to my recent pieces.

containment

perhaps we need that tall wall.

perhaps we need to contain this wanton hate, our wrecked violence in

like a delinquent weaned on jealousy—

toss ourselves into a cell behind barbed wire

perhaps this regressive insistence for barbaric practices needs to be

quarantined—

this throwback to paint our bodies with mud and brush our teeth with

urine,

to burn others as ash

to use them to tan our hides.

perhaps we are too dangerous for the world—

we false pagan gods demanding

blood sacrifice of unwary innocents.

other countries can rationalize, govern themselves. we refuse to.

in a cereal box

i'm looking for the prize in this junk filled box
of pestilential chemicals and oil disguised as nutrition
"lucky" the front of the box says and yet no luck here
it's as if some orange beast dictated lies, coached conway's newspeak
i can't swallow this—it would leave me somewhere on the streets
heaving, my innards spasming, lungs unable to find clean air.
and i certainly refuse to buy this for developing children
misled them to think this is good, is a reasonable choice.
this wasn't on my list, i didn't put this in my grocery cart
it did not sneak home, hidden under california's harvest and
heartland's produce
the only thing tempting may be the much touted surprise
"you won't believe how good. it will be the best. others not good, not
good at all"
and even though i dumped it out,
sifted through the manufactured preservatives and crumbs of...
undistinguishable
any gold in this plastic bag of garbage turns out to be some cancerous
yellow dye
there is no prize to be had; only a con—already rejected.

natural

it's should be expected after election day
the weather as unsettled as i am
a frantic bite to the chilling air
in the frenetic wind there is are little chittering voices
of squirrels and winter birds in revolt
a tiny brown bird hides among the bare branches in the ornamental
plum
she could be a stub of a broken branch if you don't focus, don't discern

her exclamations are the sounds of twigs breaking, nuts falling to the
ground
shells breaking too soon on the exposed bricks
there are apples still left on the huddled apple tree,
the fruit left for wintering creatures unable to hibernate
perhaps i should have harvested them, hoarded and preserved them—
there will be need—but the world is dying
there will be starvation, and sickness, water polluted with oil—
and i want to be able to feed it still, even in some small way
so...this dun bird, neighboring squirrels, nocturnal raccoons
even the ants and the worms that will feast on their corpse cores
we custodians are failing—the air is punctuated
with strident crows' screeching—a murder that is what it is
murdering white crows perched on telephone lines, power lines
"nevermore" they parrot victoriously "nevermore..." as frozen rain
drops down
ripples forming, multiplying in puddles
divots being left in graveled mud.